The Midnight Ghost

The Midnight Ghost

In The Haunted Castle

Master Samarth Nair

White Falcon
Publishing

www.whitefalconpublishing.com

The Midnight Ghost
Master Samarth Nair

Published by
White Falcon Publishing, Chandigarh, India

ISBN - 978-81-19510-01-6

TABLE OF CONTENTS

Chapter 1

Mysterious Memories

The silence of the Chicago River was a point of attraction that evening. William was still feeling thoughtful. "Quit gnawing your fingernails," instructed Scwarez. William was frightened. Tapping on his shoulder, Scwarez said, "I think the breeze of the stream is taking more time for our strange recollections. I feel that you are still in Hot Springs." "Indeed, I have obviously never envisioned that I will escape from the appalling hands of those beasts." "The ravishing beauty of that crown is there in my mind," said Scwarez.

The sun was bidding adieu to another day. The two detectives were watching the beauty of the sun hiding behind the horizon. "I forgot to tell you something," Scwarez broke the silence. "Yesterday I read in the newspaper that the crown is there in the Townsville Museum". "Goodness, it's so close to us. Will we make any arrangements to visit the gallery to revive the puzzling recollections?" "That is really smart," Scwarez promptly concurred. "However, we need to check with Roger and Marlin regardless of whether they are free tomorrow."

While strolling by the side of the river, the crown, Hot Springs, and the ship Mariana flashed across their mind.

The door of the beautifully painted apartment flung open. A bold man with a French beard invited William and Scwarez with an expansive grin. "Hope you enjoyed the evening near the river. I know that the cool breeze will help William rejuvenate his mind and overcome his past thoughts." William grinned. He was about to say something when Scwarez interrupted, "Are you free tomorrow? Shall we visit the museum to see the crown?" "Hahaha, are you still after that crown? It's been ages since we have solved that mystery." "But it still haunts our minds," replied Marlin. "You are here? We were just going to ask about you," Scwarez said. Marlin inquisitively inquired, "Is there any other mystery to be solved?" "Maybe tomorrow we may get an answer; a detective's life is incomplete without mysteries. My subconscious mind is whispering to me that something is going to happen tomorrow. So, get ready for another mystery. Our plan is fixed. We are going to the museum tomorrow." Marlin looked outside the window and said, "The round moon is silently witnessing what we have decided."

TOWNSVILLE
MUSEUM

Chapter 2

THE SHOCKING SURPRISE

The sun peeped through the window. One more day had unfolded, carrying with it new expectations and goals. The light of the daybreak oozed into the room. Scwarez rubbed his sleepy eyes and moved to the window. There was a silvery shine overhead.

Marlin was curiously searching for something. Roger enthusiastically inquired, "What are you searching for?" "I have misplaced my camera somewhere, since we are going to the museum today, I thought we might need it." Roger taunted him, "Hey fool, they won't allow you to take photos. There will be tight security. You will be flabbergasted on seeing the precious things you have never seen in your lifetime." Marlin thoughtfully replied, "So, if we steal at least one precious thing, we won't need to work for a lifetime, right?" Roger's reply made everyone laugh. "You need not have to work outside, but you have to work inside the prison."

William was the first to get ready for the visit. His mind was loaded up with considerations about the crown.

The gigantic structure of the Townville museum welcomed the young detectives. The magnificent towers were enough to evoke anyone's curiosity. There was a huge crowd outside the museum. William was frantic. "Why such a crowd? How will we get inside?" The siren of the police van hovered around the museum. Scwarez said, "Something is wrong. Let's go and inquire."

A tall man with a dubious look approached them. "Hope you came here to visit the museum. But you won't be allowed to enter the museum today." "What!" exclaimed Roger. "The police have sealed the place," the man continued. "For what?" Marlin was curious to know the reason. "Some theft has occurred. But what exactly was stolen even I am not sure." The man went away. All the four detectives were standing by the side of their car with all their hopes shattered. Marlin noticed that someone from the crowd was observing them. He whispered to Roger, "Hey, look at that man in uniform. He seems to be a staff of the museum. He is watching us for a long time now." Scwarez gathered courage and moved toward the person. The man was exceptionally eager to see Scwarez. "Are you the Incredible Four who solved the mystery behind a crown that was lost for ages?" "Yes, of course, how do you know about that?"

"The same crown is there in this museum and I'm the curator of the museum."

"OH, great! So, can you help us enter the museum?" asked Scwarez. "Sorry, it's not possible today. Last night, the precious necklace of the Queen of Spain from 15th century, which was on display in this museum, was stolen." "Oh, it's so disappointing," Scwarez replied in a sad tone.

Scwarez narrated the whole incident to his friends. When they were about to enter into their car, William pointed to someone and said, "Someone is signaling us to stop the car." Scwarez looked back. "Oh, it's the same curator. I think he needs us." The curator approached them and asked Scwarez, "I need to talk to you. When will you be free? Where should I come?"

"Sure, we will be free in the evening. Let's meet at Saville Restaurant in the north of Townsville at 6 o' clock." He nodded and quietly moved away. Roger was inquisitive. "Why does he want to meet us? Is it something related to the necklace? But the police are already inquiring about the case. What is our role in that?" Marlin retorted, "Don't be in a hurry. We will wait till evening."

Chapter 3

A STRANGE MEETING

It was a cold evening. The setting sun cast long shadows on the ground. The inclining beams of the sunset gave an orange border to the sky. The pale moon sparkled like a shimmering hook in the sky.

Scwarez gazed towards the blanket of stars. The Saville Restaurant was cozy and rich, with a faintly lit space loaded up with two-seater tables, a huge piano that was waiting for the gentle touch of the pianist, and a whole divider that was a gigantic painting of a Barbarian-style castle.

All four of them sat in a little corner. William restlessly drank the water when it showed up. He was apprehensive. He mumbled to himself, "Was this a trap carefully plotted by the curator?" "Order please," a faint low voice interrupted them. "Four espressos and some chocolate cookies," Marlin initiated to place the order. Scwarez's eyes were hooked at the entrance of the restaurant. "Where is the curator? He is not at all punctual," grumbled Roger. They heard heavy footsteps from behind. "I have been waiting for you for so long," they heard an unusual voice. All four detectives turned back; it was an impulsive action. The tall man with a broad smile was standing behind them. "I forgot to introduce myself to you in the morning as I was tensed. I'm Sam Parker. I have been working in the Townsville Museum for the past 8 years." Scwarez greeted him and offered him a seat. The aroma of the expressos tickled their nostrils. "Shall I order you an espresso?" Roger asked. Sam nodded, "But no sugar and no cream." "Strange taste," Marlin remarked. "That does not please my palette," replied Sam.

William was still lost in thoughts. He curiously asked, "Why did you want to meet us?" "I hope you have some time to listen to me." "Yes, of course we do," replied Scwarez. "As I told you in the morning, the necklace of the Spanish queen was stolen last night. As I am an employee of the museum and I was working during those hours, the management suspended me from the service till the culprit was caught. As I am badly in need of my job, I request you to investigate this case. I have read that you solved the case of the crown very intelligently. I was fascinated by the way you unfolded the mystery. I expect you to do the same in this case too."

Marlin, Roger, and William looked at Scwarez for his reply. Scwarez extended his hands to Sam and they exchanged hands. "Yes, we are ready for the mission."

Sam confidently smiled. Marlin asked, "Can you share with us the picture of the necklace so that we can get an idea about it?" "Sure," he handed over an envelope. "You can go through this whenever you are free." And then, they parted. Roger sighed, "Yet another mystery."

Chapter 4

THE STOLEN NECKLACE

The busy roads of the day gave way to silent paths at night. The dimly lit street light remarked the end of a day. William was very silent as though he was desperate because he couldn't see the crown as planned by them yesterday.

Marlin shouted, "Scwarez, where is that envelope? I would like to see the necklace." Scwarez was talking to someone on the phone. He gestured to Marlin to maintain silence as he could not hear what the other person was saying. Roger was busy in the kitchen with his usual experiments.

"Dinner is ready!" shouted Roger. Except William, the rest of them were at the table. "Where is our thinker, William?" inquired Marlin. "I think he is still behind the crown, not the necklace," replied Roger. "You cannot mock me all you want. The crown changed my life, so how can I forget about it?" said William while approaching the dining table.

The dinner included steak and tomato sandwiches. The hot spicy and juicy tomatoes stimulated the hunger of the four intellectuals. Marlin was the first to munch on the sandwich. "Wow... Delicious... Roger, you are an expert cook." Scwarez was lost in his thoughts. "Who were you talking to on the phone?" asked Marlin. "Oh...that was my friend. He was asking me whether I had heard about the theft at the museum." "Did you say we are going to investigate the case?" "Not at all; we should not disclose that to anyone. It ought to be kept discreet." "My mind is around the curator," Roger said. "Why have they suspended him from service? Maybe he is involved in that theft." However, Marlin supported Sam by saying, "If he is involved in the theft, then why did he approach us to solve the case?" Scwarez intruded, "We shouldn't indiscriminately pass judgment on anybody without having proof. Finish your dinner quickly and join me. I will open the envelope." "Sure, we're prepared," Marlin enthusiastically answered.

The green-colored envelope was waiting for the detectives on their side-table. The leader of the group silently opened the envelope. The other three were standing around the table. They were astounded to see the image of the exquisite necklace. On the back of the photo, there was a description about the necklace. Scwarez read it loudly:

"This necklace belonged to the Queen of Spain in the 15th century. She was known as Queen Margarine.

Once, the kingdom was attacked by the neighboring kingdom. She escaped the palace and the necklace now belonged to the other kingdom. They gave it to the other members of the family who safeguarded it until on March 30,1946, when it was presented to the Townsville Museum to keep it safe as a family heirloom for the kingdom. It is kept there even till today. The necklace was kept in a jewelry box with wooden carvings. The shimmering green stones and the stunning jewels added to the excellence of the necklace."

Marlin exclaimed, "Wow, so elegant! Now I understand why the thief has stolen it – to adorn the neck of his beautiful wife." "Don't act silly," Scwarez reminded him. "It is very expensive. The person who has stolen it will be able to survive through his lifetime with that money."

"That means the robbery was well-planned," said Marlin. While all the others were comfortably sleeping, Scwarez couldn't sleep that night. He was thinking of all the possibilities of the theft. The dim light in Scwarez and Roger's room disturbed Roger's sleep. He saw that Scwarez was searching something in the morning newspaper. Roger curiously inquired what he was searching for in the newspaper. Scwarez replied, "Obviously, I am searching whether the news of the theft has reached the newspaper. But I found something more intriguing than the theft of the necklace."

"What is it?" Roger wondered. Scwarez handed over the paper to him. He glanced at the news and was shocked. "My goodness, that's quite strange," he shouted. "Yes, my mind is revolving around this news now instead of the stolen necklace."

Chapter 5

A New Expedition

The sun's rays slightly patted William and Marlin as they were in profound rest. The chirping of birds distracted their sleep. Marlin stretched his hands as though he got a peaceful sleep. Suddenly, he noticed that Scwarez and Roger were seriously discussing something. He slowly went to them and asked them the topic of discussion. Scwarez said, "There is something quite interesting in the paper. Have a look." Marlin was quite shocked once he finished reading the article. "Do you think that ghosts are real?" "I don't think that they exist in this world." "But then how is all this happening in Ferdinand's mansion?"

William overheard their conversation and he rushed to the spot. "What happened to Ferdinand's castle?" Scwarez took the lead while he explained. "There was shocking news in yesterday's evening newspaper that in Willington, Spain, there is a castle on the top of the tallest of The Six Hills. It belonged to Ferdinand, a rich merchant. Now, his grandchildren are the heirs of the property. But, for the past year, it has been deserted as his grandchildren are working in faraway places. The people near the castle cannot live peacefully nowadays as they are witnessing a ghost at midnight looming in the area near the castle. Hence, people are afraid to go near the castle even during daytime. Most of the people are evacuating the place because of that midnight ghost."

"It sounds very bizarre," said William. "How is this happening? They are supernatural beings and do not exist in the world. Maybe it is a belief. What is your opinion, Scwarez?" "I think there is a mystery behind the midnight ghost. May god bless us so that we can meet and greet the midnight ghost. Maybe that ghost will be our host for the next few days."

"What do you mean? I don't understand. Are you going to stay there?" asked Roger. "Not me alone. 'We' are going to stay there if the owner of the castle permits." Marlin suddenly replied, "I have some family commitments, so I'll be going to my home today." "Hahaha," laughed Roger. "The midnight ghost is waiting for four of us, not three. So, be ready for the expedition; no more excuses." William was very upset when he saw Marlin's desperate face. "Are you really afraid of ghosts, my friend?" Marlin silently looked at them.

Scwarez meddled, "Yesterday you asked me whom I was talking to on the phone. It was my friend who has a farmhouse near that castle. But, for the past few months, he cannot go there and do his business because of this midnight ghost. He was seeking my help to solve that issue." "Then, what did you say?" asked Roger. "I told him that I can solve the issues created by human beings, not ghosts. But he showed a lot of trust in me. So, I thought I should look into the matter seriously."

Marlin had doubts about his choice. "What about the necklace? Who will take that case? Did you make false promises to Sam that you will help him? Why did you do so?"

"We'll take both the cases. If I have made a promise, I shall fulfil it. But all that I need is your support." "We are there with you always," chorused all three. "So today we are going to Willington to meet the midnight ghost. Get ready for another adventure."

Chapter 6

An Adventurous Journey

"We're already getting late. Come on. Hurry up, fast. Pack your essentials and get ready," Scwarez instructed the others. "Are we going today?" enquired William. "Yes, of course. My friend has made all necessary arrangements for our stay. But we should reach the farmhouse before 6 pm as it's a hilly area. The place will be covered by mist after six and we will not be able to find the spot precisely. Moreover, driving through the hairpin bends at night will be a tedious task. So, we should hurry up now." Roger was the first to get into the car. William and Scwarez were discussing the route to the place.

"Where is Marlin?" shouted Roger. "Perhaps, he is looking for his camera, which is his perfect partner." Marlin hesitatingly came to the car. Scwarez handed over the key to Marlin and said, "You're an expert driver. So, come on. Only you'll be able to complete this task."

There were different thoughts in everyone's mind when the wheels started rolling. The scorching sun disturbed their adventurous journey. They thought about taking a rest for a while as all of them were tired. They took an afternoon nap as they had forgotten the warning given by Scwarez's friend, Alveres.

"Trrrrrrringggg!!!!" The phone ring distracted their sleep. "Who is there?" Scwarez asked in a feeble voice. "Where are you? I am your friend, Alveres. I've already warned you to reach my farmhouse before six as it's dangerous to travel through that abandoned way."

"Yes, we've crossed the signboard saying '5 km to Celery Town'.

"Oh, still there? That means you're not seriously taking my warning. You're not going to reach here by 6 o'clock."

"Actually, we took a nap in between. That's why our journey got delayed. Anyhow we will try to reach fast." Roger was feeling refreshed after the short nap and he wished to drink a hot cup of coffee to refresh himself. He enquired to a passerby whether there was any café near them.

"You should take a deviation. 1 km to the left," said the man. Scwarez agreed with Roger because all three of them were badly in need of a coffee.

The vibe of The Four Coffees Café and the dark tables perfectly organized called them in from the abandoned way. They ventured into the bistro and requested four coffees. Roger glanced around. "It appears to me that the café is solely for us. Nobody is there around us." Within no time, the hot aromatic coffee was there in front of them. The man who served the coffee gave an expansive grin, which showed his yellow teeth. William was eager to talk to the waiter. He asked, "Why is there nobody here?" "We don't have enough customers in the evening as travelling through this place is unsafe. Maybe you know that. Where is your destination? Hope it is nearby. Or else we'll arrange your stay here since it is risky outside," the waiter said in one breath.

Roger interrupted, "No thanks, our destination is nearby." Marlin extended a fearful look at Roger. Roger tried to change Marlin's mood by pointing outside. "Your camera is waiting for the good scenery of this place. Go and capture it, fast."

Marlin was amazed to see the wrinkled hills covered with snow. Deafening silence surrounded him. The air was chilling. The peaks were drenched in the dazzling light of sunset. As usual, the sun didn't forget to hide that day too.

"Marlin!!!" screamed William. "It's time to move."

"Again 5 km… it's already getting dark. I am worried whether we will reach there safely or not." Marlin aroused his doubt.

"Be brave. We are detectives, we should never be afraid." Scwarez said confidently.

To their bad fortune, it started drizzling and they found it difficult to continue their journey. They called Alveres for help. He said he could not come to that place because it was raining and his vehicle was not in a good condition. They understood that it was an excuse and he was trying to neglect their request.

The night was getting darker and thicker. All the four were trapped inside the car. They searched for some shelter but in vain. They could hear only the howling wind and strange noises of the animals. The deserted road was waiting for the company of streetlights. Pitter patter raindrops hit on the dark-glass windowpane. Somehow, they managed to start their car but couldn't move for another 1 km. They felt that there was some obstacle in the midst of the road but couldn't see properly what exactly it was. "Is it a tree that tumbled down?" asked Marlin. "I think it's a man in a raincoat," said Roger. "No, it's a wild fox," argued William. Scwarez gathered courage to open the door and check what it was, but his friends didn't allow him to do so.

Chapter 7

In the Farm House

Scwarez neglected his friends' words and moved toward the gigantic figure. The remaining three were curious about what would happen next. While Scwarez was moving near the figure, the remaining three gasped and closed their eyes. They were expecting some strange noises but nothing happened. Because of the thick mist, they couldn't figure out what exactly happened to Scwarez. "He vanished into the darkness," Marlin exclaimed. William said, "No, he is approaching us." Roger added, "Something is there in his hand." Scwarez knocked at the car door. Roger was eager to know what he had in his hand so he quickly opened the door. It was a dark branch of a tree. Scwarez said, "See here, for this you all were creating the humdrums. I think because of the wind, this branch fell down from the nearby tree. Marlin's guess was correct."

"Is there any possibility to escape from this place?" asked Marlin. "The road is fully blocked and it is not possible to move from here today. Maybe, by tomorrow morning, we will be able to reach the farmhouse. But, today, we should rest in the car."

Tiny dew drops were dancing in the sunlight of the dawn. The rain had quenched the thirst of all the flora and fauna of the place. The leaves were dancing as the morning breeze patted them. The road was crisp and clear. All four of them were ready to go to the farmhouse. Within half an hour, they reached the farmhouse. They saw Alveres waiting for them at the gate. He apologized for not helping them last night. He even informed them that he was not there in the farmhouse yesterday as every night, he went to his cousin's house in a faraway place in order to escape from the midnight ghost. His family has been staying with his cousin for the past few months.

A lean man with a bony frame came near them. Alveres introduced him to the detectives. "Meet Carlo. He is the caretaker of the farmhouse. He will take care of all your needs." He instructed Carlo in a strange language to assist them and to take them to their rooms.

Roger opened the dusty window of his room. He could see fluffy clouds taking strange shapes. He could see an unclear image of a deserted castle. "Who is staying there?" he asked Carlo. "Oh, that is Ferdinand's castle. He was a rich merchant. His wife passed away when his son was 6 years old. He raised his son alone without anyone's help. His son married a rich man's daughter. They had two children. Theirs was a happy and contented family, but their happiness didn't last long. The villain entered their life in the form of a car accident and both Ferdinand's son and his wife died on the spot and the grandchildren escaped miraculously. The responsibility of the grandchildren came into Ferdinand's hand. After a few years, he also passed away because of old age and nobody knows where his grandchildren are. For the past year, nobody has visited that castle and it is completely locked. But people saw strange figures resembling Ferdinand's son and daughter-in-law during the night. People believe that they are their ghosts because they passed away without fulfilling their wishes and it was an untimely death. Don't open this window as there will be scary noises and strange sights outside at midnight.

After hearing this description, Roger exclaimed, "That sounds interesting. Is it possible to visit the castle?" "No way, sir. It is completely locked and no one knows where Ferdinand's grandchildren are."

Meanwhile, Marlin entered the room. He said, "I've heard the description of the castle. I'm slightly afraid." Roger replied," Ferdinand's son and daughter-in-law have no intention to kill people. They only want to show everyone their presence. That's what I could understand from his description. So, don't worry and be ready to meet them tonight."

Chapter 8

A Horrid Night

Roger and Scwarez were walking outside. It was dark but fireflies lit the dark sky. The lights of the farmhouse switched off abruptly as though someone had done it deliberately. Roger yelled," Carlo!" Within seconds, Carlo came out with a torch. They could see each other clearly now. "What happened? Why did the lights switch off?" "There is power failure very often in this place. Or maybe due to yesterday's downpour, there might be some electrical maintenance issue. We can expect the electricity to return by tomorrow morning only as nobody will do maintenance work at night." Scwarez asked, "Where is Alveres?" "Master has gone to his cousin's house. He came to meet you when you were asleep but then thought not to disturb you. He will be back in the morning. You please get inside and have dinner. It is not safe to stand outside."

All four friends sat around the dining table. It was 10 o' clock. Triiing.... Scwarez's phone rang. "Who is that at this time?" Scwarez muttered as he was searching his phone. "Hello," he heard a feeble voice from the other end. "Hope you remember me. This is Sam." "Yes, the necklace is there in my mind and we are after it and very soon we'll find the culprit; you don't worry and sleep peacefully." "I feel optimistic after talking to you. May god bless you to solve the case soon. My prayers and wishes are there with you."

Scwarez scratched his head and returned to the dining table. Everybody was silent. Roger broke the silence, "That was a lie! I didn't expect that from you." Scwarez smiled and said, "Who said I'm not thinking about the necklace? Yesterday also, I was searching the whereabouts of the necklace and the people associated with it. But I didn't involve you. Once the time comes, I will let you know everything."

All of them, except Roger, went to bed. He was thinking about Ferdinand's son and daughter-in-law. He was sitting in a big armchair beside a fireplace. His eyes were waiting for sleep's gentle touch. But he couldn't wink his eye as somebody was whispering to him that something would happen at midnight. He slowly moved upstairs with a candle. Somebody touched his shoulder. He suddenly turned back and the candle tumbled down from his grip. The person behind him showed the flashlight of his mobile. It was Carlo. "Oh, you! Why are you behind me?" Roger was a little annoyed. "I thought you are in need of my help because all the others are sleeping and you're still awake." "It seems that you want me to sleep fast," Roger whispered to himself. The clock struck twelve. Carlo handed over another candle to Roger.

Roger instructed Carlo to go away and not disturb him. He slowly and steadily moved to the first floor where the others were sleeping. He gently pushed open the door of their bedrooms and noticed that all were in deep sleep. All the windows were closed except one. The to and fro of the windowpane evoked curiosity in Roger. There was strong wind outside. The flowers spread fragrance throughout the room. He glanced through the window. He couldn't see the castle clearly because of the mist but he saw a shadow of a tall figure outside the castle. He heard the wailing sound of a dog. His eyes groped in darkness to search for the dog. He went in search of his binoculars. To his surprise, when he came back, somebody had locked the window. He rushed toward the stairs because he heard some footsteps.

He thought it was Carlo so he moved toward Carlo's room and was shocked to see Carlo sleeping comfortably. He rushed back again and tried to open the window but in vain.

With a lot of anxiety and curiosity in his mind, he went to bed. A lot of questions popped up in his mind. Whose shadow was there near the castle? From where had he heard the dog's moaning sound? How was the windowpane locked? Who had done that? All the questions remained unanswered in his mind. He was perplexed whether he should tell all his experiences to his friends or not? Perhaps they will taunt him. Eventually, he slipped into sleep.

Chapter 9

An Unusual Sight

The chilled morning gave Roger energy to go for a stroll. He intentionally decided to go near the castle as the thoughts about the shadow and the dog were drifting around him. He thought that he needed some clarity and then only would he reveal the matter to his friends. The abandoned building shone golden in the light of the rejuvenating day. Roger felt that the gigantic pillars were witnessing all that happened at midnight yesterday. The fallen leaves on the ground marked the presence of gushy wind. The bloomy gate with an amazing design proved that it had spent years in solitude. While he was at the entrance, somebody called him. When he turned back, he saw Alveres gesturing him to go back to the farmhouse. Without lingering too much, he walked back. "Why did you go there?" asked Alveres. "To see the midnight ghost," Roger scornfully replied. "What! Are you crazy?" Roger smiled.

The morning meal embellished the dining table. The steaming pot of tea and farm fresh food gave an ornamental look to the breakfast. All the three were patiently waiting for Roger. "Where have you been?" asked William. "Just to admire the beauty of Ferdinand's castle," replied Roger. Carlo was readily serving them breakfast. Roger asked him, "Is there a pet dog here?" "Dog? My master is allergic to dogs' fur. So, we're not having any dogs. Down that valley, there is an old lady's house. She has a dog. You might have seen her. She usually comes here in the morning to do work on the farm. We lost a few cows and goats due to midnight ghosts. That's why my master is worried."

Scwarez and Roger thought of visiting their farm in the backyard. There they saw a grey-haired woman who was talking to the cows. She wore white glasses with a pink gown. A red purse was lying beside the cows, probably her bag. She looked white and bleak and wore sandals. They tried talking to her but she didn't give a reply. Instead, she frowned at them. An enormous black Scottish Terrier was giving them a terrifying look that made them shudder.

Roger expressed his doubt to Scwarez, "Is it true that dogs can see ghosts at night? That's why they're howling at night?" "What happened to you? Did you hear a howl last night?" "No, just confirming."

That day went without much hue and wonder. Roger was completely lost in his anticipation and was eagerly waiting for that night.

As usual, everyone went to sleep at 10 o'clock, except Roger. He was waiting for the shadow and the dog's howl. He made up his mind to go to the castle at midnight. The clock struck twelve. He stepped out of the farmhouse. His nightgown swayed due to the gushy wind. To his surprise, he saw the shadow of a man wearing a long overcoat near the gate of the castle. He gathered courage to go near that figure. It was terribly dark around. He could hear some footsteps. At first, he thought it was his own footsteps but then he realized that somebody was following him. He turned back. "Huhhh. Gracious! Scwarez, you were following me?" "Yes. Yesterday, I noticed a change in you, so I decided to follow you. I don't want you to be in trouble." Roger enthusiastically pointed to the shadow of the man. But Scwarez couldn't see anything there. "Maybe he might have gone inside," Roger said. "I firmly believe that he is a man and not a ghost. Why is he coming here every midnight? Who is that man?" He posed a lot of questions but Scwarez didn't reply. "Shall we go near the gate?" Scwarez nodded. They saw that the big lock of the gate had vanished and it was slightly open. The screeching sound of the gate awakened the dog who was sleeping peacefully there. He started to bark loudly. Both were frightened. Roger took out a biscuit from his bag and gave it to him. He quietened. They intruded into the compound of the castle. The windowpane of one of the rooms was slightly open. They both peeped through the window. "Wow, so astonishing! Every thing is kept intact! How is it possible?" Roger was amazed." Carlo said that for the past one year, nobody has visited the castle. Then who is keeping the castle so clean and dust-free? I was expecting a cobwebbed place."

The room was kept neat and clean. There were beautiful carvings on the ceiling. The bed was tidy. There were two big portraits. One showed a man with a long white beard, elf-like ears, and a smile. Underneath it, was written: Joseph Ferdinand. The other showed a picture of a young man with a brown moustache, a smug face, and dirty look, and underneath it was written: Arnold Ferdinand. When the two peered around the room, they saw another portrait but of a lady. Her hair was brown-black and it flowed over the shoulders. She wore an elegant gown bordered with golden laces and underneath it was written: Elizabeth Ferdinand.

They heard somebody running through the corridor. When they followed the footsteps, they saw a womanly figure wearing a gown resembling the one that Arnold's wife, Elizabeth, was wearing. They could not see the face clearly because she was wearing a scarf. Suddenly, something jumped over them. They hit the ground and fainted.

Chapter 10

THE STRANGE FIGURE IN THE GRAVE

William and Marlin were shocked to see that Roger and Scwarez were not in their room. They searched the whole farmhouse but couldn't find them. Then suddenly, one young boy who used to come to the farmhouse for milking the cows came panting towards them. He shouted, "Carlo!" "What's the matter?" "I have seen two dead people near the castle. Please come and see." A shudder of fear ran down the spine of William and Marlin. They uttered, "Scwarez and Roger..." They rushed towards the place as fast as a speeding train. As soon as they reached there, they understood that the boy was exaggerating and they had fainted and nothing more had happened to them. They sprinkled water on their face. It was Scwarez who opened his eyes first. Suddenly, he turned toward Roger and began trying waking him up. William was the first to inquire, "How did you came here?" Roger was about to narrate the incident but Scwarez interrupted in between as Carlo and the young boy were there. He said," We have enough time to discuss all this. First, let us take some rest."

All four detectives were in a room. William and Marlin were silent. Scwarez understood that they were disappointed. So, he tried to pacify them by narrating all the incidents of last night. They were astounded to hear them. They assured Scwarez and Roger that they would extend their full support to solve this mystery and that they were longing to witness the incidents at night. All four decided to observe the place throughout the day.

As they were walking outside, some supernatural powers were attracting them towards the castle. They went to the place where the womanly figure vanished last night.

There, in the center of the compound, was a huge tree that was leaning towards two graves. It seemed as though there was a divine connection between the tree and the departed souls. As soon as the four detectives reached the spot, they could feel the wind whispering to them that the departed souls are unhappy.

As they moved forward, the rustle of the dried leaves crushing under their feet reminded them that the place was abandoned, but the next moment, they saw two fresh roses on the graves. They felt that the dew drops on the flowers had some story to tell them.

They noticed that two eyes were watching them… They didn't speak to each other. An eerie silence spread across the place. That night was indeed crucial for them as they had already made up their mind to visit the place at midnight.

The clock struck twelve. All four gathered their courage to meet the midnight ghost. They silently moved out of the farmhouse. They stationed at a place from where they could easily get a glimpse of Ferdinand's castle and the graves. The gushy wind rattled the dried leaves near the grave. An owl was sitting on a branch of the lonely tree near the grave and was hooting as though it was signaling someone to come to the place.

The dim light of the moon was the only light in that place. There was deafening silence and the only sound they could hear was their heartbeats.

They heard the usual footsteps. Their eyes were searching for the tall man and the old woman. Roger broke the silence and shouted, "Look over there!" Scwarez signaled him to be quiet. They heard a screeching sound. They tried to see the face of the man, but it was a futile attempt. The gigantic tree was protecting him by giving him ample space to hide. They were eager to know what was that screeching sound but because of the mist they couldn't see clearly. However, they saw that he was opening a grave and within no time he vanished.

Within seconds, the fragrance of incense sticks reached them. Soon, they blacked out.

The rays of the sun patted them. "What happened to us? Where are we?" asked William. They rushed to the farmhouse.

Carlo, with a scornful smile, greeted them and asked them, "Did you see that Arnold and his wife opening the grave at the castle and entering into it?" Marlin curiously asked, "How do you know that?" "That is the usual sight here and people are afraid of them. That's why we're saying this place is under the control of the midnight ghosts." Scwarez smiled. "Let's see. We'll try to bring them in the morning." Carlo was shocked to hear this. Nobody was uttering a single word.

All four friends were deep in thoughts. William was anxious. "We have seen the tall man going inside the grave. Then where did he go? Why didn't he return?" Roger shared his view. "Maybe there is an underground passage in the grave or we didn't see him when he came back. Of course, I cannot remember anything after he went inside." "Same with me," agreed William. "For me too," said Marlin. "That means something was there in the air that made us sleep. I could smell the fragrance of incense sticks once he opened the grave. Maybe that air was toxic and acted as a villain yesterday. That was why we all slept unknowingly." "Great! Arnold is quite intelligent. Somebody is informing him about our actions," William inferred. "I have doubts about Carlo. He is always after us," said Roger. "Don't share false speculations," said Scwarez. "We want solid proof. My subconscious mind is whispering to me that we'll catch the midnight ghost tonight."

Chapter 11

Mystery Inside the Castle

They heard some noises outside. It was Alveres arguing with the old lady. "What's the matter?" inquired Scwarez. "She needs sleep. If she is not there, who will take care of my cows? I have lost many cows and goats because of midnight ghosts and if nobody is there to take care of them, I will lose the rest too. But she is so adamant that she won't come. What should I do?" replied Alveres. "Why does she need sleep?" "She says she is planning to go to her home but I don't think that's correct. She has a dog and many other pets. If she is not there, who will take care of them? I think she is giving lame excuses."

They saw that William was mumbling something. "What happened to you?" asked Marlin. "The tall man whom we met yesterday, near the grave resembled someone very familiar to us but I can't figure out who precisely. Is it Alveres or is it Carlo or the boy who came for milking the cows?" Roger mocked at him by saying, "Or is it Scwarez?"

Marlin suggested," Shall we inform the police?" Scwarez said," What will we tell them, that we have seen ghosts? The police can catch thieves, not ghosts." "But we're sure that they're not ghosts," doubted Marlin. "Yes, but only we know that. We should catch them red-handed." "That will remain a dream, as they are better trained than us," said Marlin. "Don't lose hope, we will catch them," Scwarez was confident.

That night, they made a plan. Two of them would stay near the graves and the other two would take a different position so that the fragrance of incense sticks does not attack them. Roger and Scwarez took a position a little far from the grave; Marlin and William were at that good old spot where they stood last night. Things happened as usual. The screeching sound of the grave reminded them of last night. This time, they were all extra-cautious but the same thing happened to Marlin and William as soon as the fragrance of incense sticks started to spread. They fell down. But that was not the case for Roger and Scwarez. They saw the figure moving inside and closing the lid. After a few minutes, they saw a womanly figure moving around the castle. The black dog was wailing. She gently opened the door of the castle and went inside. After a while, they saw the man in a black coat also going inside the castle.

They silently moved toward the castle and peeped through the window. They saw that the dining table was neatly kept. The room was dark but the lady was lighting the candle-lights. She looked exactly like Elizabeth.

The detectives were holding their breath and waiting to see the man. They heard a serious voice inquiring," Is everything ready?" The footsteps of the man were coming closer. There was a box in his hand that he took from the grave. They understood that the lady was insisting that he open the box. "What is inside the box?" asked Scwarez. "Maybe he had brought some gifts for his wife." When he opened the box, they couldn't believe their eyes. That was the same necklace that was stolen from the museum! The dazzling light of the necklace illuminated the place. The man was standing in front of Arnold's photo. "What is he doing? Is he praying for forgiveness for his sins? Why is he not turning?"

"Trrrrringg..." rang Scwarez's phone. The man was startled. Suddenly, he turned around. They were shocked to see the man. He was so familiar to them. Without a second thought, they gasped and fled from their place with their mouths wide open with sheer shock and disbelief. Their faces were as pale as death. They thought that the man was behind them. They tried their level best to hide themselves without being caught.

Chapter 12

A Misleading Thought

They didn't have the courage to look for Marlin and William. "How is this possible? That man was pretending in front of us. How can it be? He's a good actor," said Roger. After a while, they heard someone knocking on the door of the farmhouse. They were frightened. They thought that he was following them. Then, they heard a familiar voice in a feeble manner, "Open the door; we're here." "Yes, it is William. Maybe, they also saw the man." They rushed to open the door. William and Marlin were panting for breath. "Did you see the man?" asked Scwarez. "Yes, we were shocked and frozen; we couldn't walk. Somehow, we managed to get up from the spot," replied Marlin. "Scwarez, why are you not saying anything?" "We had seen the necklace and the man who had stolen it". "Then, what are you waiting for? We should inform the police right now," said William. Scwarez disagreed with him. "That means you're protecting the curator, Sam," Marlin replied in a desperate tone. "No way.

We should meet him today. Then, we'll come to the conclusion whether he is the culprit or not." "Still?" asked William. "We saw him."

"Let us talk to Sam. If he had seen us, he would have tried every means to harm us. Anyhow, we will talk to him today." Saying this, Scwarez rang up Sam. But he didn't pick the call. Then, they were sure that Sam had seen them. "Actually, what we're doing is wrong. He will try to escape with the necklace. Then, we won't be able to catch him. The culprit is so close to us. Scwarez, why are you behaving like this? More than this, what evidence do you need?" asked Marlin. Scwarez advised him," Don't panic, be patient."

The phone bell interrupted their discussion. "Yes, it is Sam," Scwarez said. "He is so courageous and cunning; that's why he called us," judged Roger. As soon as Scwarez picked up his call, Sam said, "I was sleeping as last night I couldn't sleep due to some disturbances. Any positive news?" inquired Sam. "Yes, within two days, we will share some happy news. Do you have time to meet with us today?" inquired Scwarez. "Sure, I'm free," replied Sam. "Please come to Willington. There is a farmhouse near to Celery Town that is owned by a man called Alveres." "Oh, I know that place very well as my grandfather's castle is there. Maybe you might have heard of Ferdinand's castle. But we never go there as there are some problems. I will talk to you later regarding that. So, we will meet today."

"He was acting so nice. I'm sure he didn't see us last night. How courageous he is. He has agreed to meet us too. It's sure that in the evening, he'll escape from here as he has to go for night duty," said Marlin. They were eagerly waiting for Sam.

It was afternoon. The scorching sun didn't allow them to go outside and wait for Sam. They heard the sound of a car outside the farmhouse. They even heard that someone was talking to Alveres. They rushed to the entrance and informed him that he was their guest and introduced Sam to Alveres. Scwarez said, "He is the curator of the Townsville Museum." Alveres greeted him and invited him into his farmhouse. Carlo was present there with a cool juice. Sam was very thankful to Carlo as he handed over the juice to him. Meanwhile, the four friends were observing his mannerisms. Nothing suspicious of a gentleman with a pleasant smile. They were wondering how a person can exhibit dual character.

While having a sumptuous lunch, they talked about the castle. Sam gave a detailed description about the castle. He said, "My grandfather was a rich merchant and he had built that castle. My father and mother passed away at a young age in a car accident and we were taken care of by our grandfather. My brother was not here with us. He went out of the country to continue his education. I stayed with my grandfather as I was not so good in studies. But, due to old age, my grandfather also left us, leaving the huge castle with us. Neither I nor my brother can take care of this property. It was entrusted to both of us. But he is least interested in it and he prefers to work outside. I am also busy and not getting enough time to come here and take care of this castle. I have a spare key to the castle. One is with the caretaker of the castle. I have not even seen him all these years. My brother had appointed him and all the dealings are done via phone as he cannot come here."

"If you want to see, I will take you there. But at nighttime, it is not safe to go there as people are seeing my ancestor's ghosts wandering there. Though, I don't believe in all that. Instead, I'm afraid of nocturnal animals because, one evening when I visited the castle, I was attacked by a bat. It was so huge that I felt that it was a man in a black coat. Then, I blacked out and early morning when I woke up, everything was intact. We could even hear the moaning sound of hounds at night. So, it's better to visit the place now."

With a lot of curiosity, they went to the castle. Sam took the lead. He opened the gigantic gate of the castle. As soon as he opened the gate, he moved to the left to visit his father's and mother's graves. He silently stood near the grave. The large tree was swaying as though the departed souls were happy to see Sam. Then they moved toward the castle. The door had a beautiful wooden carving of a dragon. They felt that this carved figure was a sign of warning not to enter the castle.

Sam was very excited to show the portraits of his grandfather, father, and mother. Marlin inquired about his brother. Sam said, "He is very much alive. As per our custom, we place the portraits of dead people in their loving memory and not of those who are alive." William inquired, "How is this castle so neat and clean?" "As I said before, there is a caretaker appointed by my brother. He will clean the castle but I don't know that man."

They introspected each and every corner of the castle with the hope of getting some clue but in vain. While they were moving out of the castle, William turned back. The castle was growing old and weak. As they silently walked, the castle stood alone, faintly saying goodbye to them.

They understood that even though they reached the farmhouse, Sam's mind was still in the castle. He was looking outside the window, watching the dark clouds. He understood that it was about to rain and if it rains, he won't be able to go as there won't be any street-lights and the place was not safe for a night drive. So, he was perplexed regarding how to get away from there. Scwarez suggested a good idea. "Tonight, you can stay here and tomorrow you can go back." But Sam didn't agree. He said that he was having some commitments and that he should go. Roger whispered, "He won't stay as he has to work at night." Marlin understood that it was Scwarez's plan to observe him. At last, Sam agreed.

It was drizzling. The tiny raindrops occupied the leaflets. The leaves were drooping because of the weight of the raindrops. The piercing gust of winds shook the trees. They were sure that Sam would find an excuse to go out at night, but to their surprise, as soon as he had his dinner he said, "I'm feeling sleepy. If you don't mind, shall I take some rest?" They agreed. But they decided to go to the castle. That night was even darker than the previous nights. Maybe due to the unexpected downpour. They were sure that the man wouldn't be there that night because he was with them and there was heavy downpour. But to their surprise, they saw the same events but with a slight difference. The man had an old umbrella. Instead of going near the grave, he straightaway moved to the castle. They saw that he was opened the castle gate and went inside. Behind him came the old woman with a dog. She also stepped inside. As usual, the man stood in front of Arnold's photo.

They saw that he was opened a small cupboard and took out the wooden box of the necklace. Pointing to the necklace, he said, "At any cost, I cannot lose this but I'm afraid that somebody is after us. I think they have visited this castle as there are signs of footprints inside the room. You take the responsibility of the necklace and keep it safe. Tomorrow, I will come here. You will then hand over the necklace to me. That will be our last deed," said the man to the old lady.

While he was handing over the box to the old lady, they saw that the man had six fingers, which was something unusual. Marlin noticed that and pointed it to everyone. He couldn't wait there for long; he wanted to check whether Sam had six fingers or not. Without waiting for his friends, he fled from there. As soon as he reached the farmhouse, he rushed upstairs. The door of Sam's room was barely closed. He jumped inside, but to his surprise, Sam was not there. He searched everywhere but he couldn't find Sam. His mind whispered to him, "At last we found the culprit."

Chapter 13

The Mystery Unfolds

With a lot of excitement, Marlin came downstairs. His heart was throbbing with delight as he was going to inform Scwarez first that Sam was missing, but he heard some conversation near the farm shed. He saw that Scwarez, William, and Roger were talking to someone. When he went near them, he was astonished. Sam was standing near the cows. "It's quite surprising to see you here," said Marlin. "Why?" asked Sam. "I had heard some peculiar sounds outside and a shadow near the farm. I thought that somebody was outside, so I came here to check that." Marlin replied, "It's okay," and extended his hand to Sam. Sam smiled. "Hand shake at midnight?" Scwarez understood that Marlin was searching for the sixth finger.

"He has only five fingers on both hands," mumbled Marlin. "What?" asked Sam. "Nothing," replied Marlin. Sam went to his room.

"Sam does not have six fingers," said Marlin to Scwarez. "Then who is that man with similar looks?" "That we should find out but we have very little time as we have all heard the man saying that he will take the necklace from there tomorrow."

The sunlight peeped into Sam's room. They heard Sam talking to someone on the phone. "Who was that?" inquired Marlin. "Ohh, that was my brother, Pam. He was there with me for the past month. He had given emotional and financial support when I lost my job. He really wished that I should find the culprit and should get back my job but that didn't happen. Tonight, he will fly to Manchester for an emergency meeting." Marlin said, "We wish to meet with him." "There is nothing to see. He is very much familiar to me as we are identical twins." William was very curious. "Then how do people recognize you both?" "We have only one difference: he has six fingers on one of his hands." Marlin sighed. "Uhhhh!!! At last!!" Scwarez smiled. Sam was surprised. "Why are you so excited?" Scwarez replied, "You'll also feel the same excitement as we bring the culprit and the necklace in front of you, tonight."

They saw that Scwarez and Roger were going out. Marlin and William understood that they were going to inform the police.

Sam was wondering how they would bring the culprit and the necklace. Lots of questions in his mind were unanswered. Anyhow, he had decided that he would wait till night.

Sam felt that something special was going to happen that night. The sky was extremely dark. He was fascinated to see the round face of the moon. He felt that the dark moments of despair and hopelessness in his life were going to an end.

Sam and Carlo were inside the farmhouse, as instructed by Scwarez. He said, "Tonight, we are going to catch the midnight ghost. Once our mission is accomplished, you will be able to see the ghost. Till that time, be safe here."

The most awaited moment arrived. All four detectives and a few police officers were there around the castle. The darkness of the night had given them a perfect hiding place. The man in the black coat came in a red fiesta car. He looked nervous. He was looked around and immediately stepped inside the castle.

The old lady and the dog arrived there on time. She had the wooden box. The dog started growling as instructed by his mistress. She was terribly frightened and silently moved toward the castle. William and Marlin went near her. She was shocked and couldn't do anything. They asked her to give them the necklace and to go inside the castle as if nothing had happened. She did as asked. The man was sitting in an armchair near the fireplace. As soon as he saw her, he was crossed. "Why are you late? I have told you the seriousness of the situation. Still, you're kidding? Where is the necklace?" He stretched his hand. His sixth finger was swaying as though he didn't like his movement. She couldn't utter a word... William and Marlin were behind her. "Can't you hear me? Are you deaf? Don't play with me; hand it over fast. I need to fly to Manchester."

"You're not going anywhere, Mr. Pam," said Scwarez loudly. "Who are you?" why are you here?" asked Pam. "We're detectives and we are investigating the case of the stolen necklace." "Which necklace? I don't know anything," defended Pam. "But we know everything," said Roger and showed him the necklace. He tried to flee from there. As soon as he reached the gate, he noticed that someone had locked it. When he turned back, He saw all four detectives and a few policemen blocking his way. He had no way to escape.

The police handcuffed him and took him out of the castle. Sam and Carlo were watching all the incidents from their room but due to the mist and darkness, they couldn't clearly see the culprit. They saw that all were coming back towards the farmhouse. Carlo opened the gate and invited them in. Scwarez went near Sam and said, "I have kept the promise." Sam anxiously looked at the man who was hiding behind the police. Sam went near him and silence prevailed in that place.

"OH NO!!!!!!!!" He screamed and burst into tears. "The right hand of mine, the one whom I had trusted more than myself, cheated me!" he yelled.

The whole place was filled with a sharp shrilling sound. He sat on the corridor unable to believe his eyes. "Why??? Why have you done this to me?"

Chapter 14

MISSION ACCOMPLISHED

The police took Pam inside and asked Carlo to give Pam and the lady a glass of water. They asked them to confess. Pam was the first to speak. "I was ambitious. I was in need of more wealth and property, but I understood that if I lead a normal life like Sam, it won't happen. So, I tried to think of crooked plans. I heard Sam talking to his wife about the necklace in the museum. I understood that my dream will be fulfilled if that necklace comes to me. So, I made plans to steal it from the museum and successfully did that. Then, I learned that this castle belonged to both of us and Sam was trying to sell this as he was in need of money. I was not at all satisfied with the share he offered me. So, I thought of the ghost's plan. I thought if I create this ghost in the minds of the neighbors, they will spread the news like wildfire. Nobody will buy the castle and even Sam won't come back here. So, I took the help of Clara who is the maid of Alveres and made a skin-mask that resembled my mother and asked her to wear it whenever she comes to help me there." "But how do the cows and goats from our shed go missing?" asked Carlo. "It was done by Clara. The toxic fragrance of incense sticks that we used to spread from the grave highly affected the animals. Some of them fainted and the rest went to sleep. Once I entered the grave, she would come here with the incense sticks and take the goats. Since they were familiar with her, and were sleepy, they would silently go with her." "You cheat!!" shouted Carlo. "How can you do this to our master?" Meanwhile Alveres entered the room as Scwarez called him.

The police took both the ghosts. Sam and Alveres thanked the officers for their timely help. William sighed, "Finally, both the mysteries solved." Roger was still lost in thoughts. "What happened to you?" inquired Marlin. "Still one more question is pestering in my mind that remains unanswered." "What's that?" asked Marlin. "While I was watching through the windowpane the first day, I went to take the binoculars and when I came back, I saw that the windowpane was locked. It was not Carlo; I saw him sleeping. But then who did that?" "Did you hear footsteps moving downstairs?" inquired Marlin. "Yes, how do you know that?" Marlin smiled and said, "It was me. I was frightened when I saw that you were looking outside and I couldn't wink my eye, so I did that." "Hahahahaha..." Laughter prevailed in that place.

Scwarez requested Sam to make arrangements in the museum so that they could see both the crown and the necklace with their full pomp and splendor. Sam agreed. The Incredible Four bid goodbye to the Midnight Ghosts and The Haunted Castle.